Acknowledgement of Land & of the Traditional Owners of this Land

I would like to acknowledge the Gadigal people of the Eora Nation, upon whose stolen land I stand on today.
I recognise that this land was never terra nullius — the land belonging to these peoples was never ceded, given up, bought or sold.
I would like to pay my respects to Aboriginal Elders past, present and emerging, and I extend this acknowledgement to all Aboriginal and Torres Strait Islander people.

Leslie

"Sound of Silence"

"Hello darkness, my old friend
I've come to talk with you again
Because a vision softly creeping
Left its seeds while I was sleeping
And the vision that was planted in my brain
Still remains
Within the sound of silence

In restless dreams, I walked alone
Narrow streets of cobblestone
'Neath the halo of a street lamp
I turned my collar to the cold and damp
When my eyes were stabbed by the flash of a neon light
That split the night
And touched the sound of silence

And in the naked light, I saw
Ten thousand people, maybe more
People talking without speaking
People hearing without listening
People writing songs that voices never shared
And no one dared
Disturb the sound of silence

"Fools" said I, *"You do not know*
Silence like a cancer grows
Hear my words that I might teach you
Take my arms that I might reach you"
But my words, like silent raindrops fell
And echoed in the wells of silence

And the people bowed and prayed
To the neon god they made
And the sign flashed out its warning
In the words that it was forming
Then the sign said, *"The words on the prophets are written on the subway walls*
In tenement halls"
And whispered in the sound of silence."

Songwriter: Paul Simon
Performed by: Simon & Garfunkel

CONTENTS

1: Pagan Street
(Via Pagana)
2: Adventures with my Father
(Avventure con mio Padre)
3: Sins of the Father
(Peccati del Padre)
4: Are you FUCKING Kidding Me?
(Mi Stai CAZZO Prendendo in Giro?)
5: I Am What I Am
(Sono Quello che Sono)
6: She Saw Me
(Lei mi ha Visto)
7: Look but Do Not Touch
(Guarda ma non Toccare)
8: I Am Not Participating
(Non sto Partecipando)
9: The Answers to Everything & Nothing
(Le Risposte a Tutto e Niente)
10: Adaptation
(Adattamento)
11: I Want YOU!
(Voglio TE!)
12: Who's Gonna Occupy This Chair?
(Chi Occuperà Questa Sedia?)
13: Rejected & Abandoned Once Again
(Rifiutato e Abbandonato di Nuovo)
14: Time to SHOUT!
(È Ora di Gridare!)
15: Peace, LO♥E & Harmony
(Pace, Amor e Armonia)
16: The Crucible
(Il Crogiolo)
17: The Last Supper
(L'ultima Cena)

CONTENTS

18: I've Got Your Back
(Ti Guardo le Spalle)
19: She Was Not a Good Friend
(Non era Una Buona Amica)
20: Time Heals All Wounds
(Il tempo Guarisce Tutte le Ferite)
21: If You Can't Make LO♥E to the One You LO♥E,
Make LO♥E to the One You're With!
*(Se non riesci a fare l'amore con colui che ami,
Fai l'AMORE con la persona con cui stai!)*
22: Why?
(Come mai?)
23: My Mother, Angela
(Mia madre, Angela)
24: I Know You're Lonely
(So che sei solo)
25: I Want to be LO♥ED
(Voglio essere Amato)
26: Cunt, is not a Dirty Word (revisited)
(Figa, non è una Sporca Parola (rivisitato))
27: Exclusivity
(Esclusività)
28: The Sex, LO♥E Dichotomy
(La Dicotomia Sesso, Amore)
29: The Third Person
(La Terza Persona)
30: The Noise of Silence
(Il Rumore del Silenzio)
31: The Power Paradox
(Il Paradosso del Potere)
32: Lean on Me
(Affidati a Me)
33: LO♥E is a Dirty Word
(L'AMORE è una Parola Sporca)

CONTENTS

34: Don't Verbal Me
(Non Parlarmi)
35: All Things Have an End
(Tutte le cose hanno una Fine)
36: I'm Gonna Use Her Words Back at Her
(Userò le Sue Sarole Contro di Lei)
37: The Future
(Il Futuro)
38: Access
(Accesso)
39: Adversity Brought Us Together
(Le Avversità ci hanno Uniti)
40: Let's Stand Naked Together
(Restiamo Nudi Insieme)
41: You are Boring
(Sei Noioso)
42: Template
(Modello)
43: I Have Clean Sheets
(Ho Lenzuola Pulite)
44: Everyone Lies
(Tutti Bugie)
45: The End
(La Fine)
46: Give Me Some Validation
(Dammi Qualche Conferma)
47: Do Not Expect Anything & Get Everything
(Non Aspettarti Nulla e Ottieni Tutto)
48: A Bohemian Life
(Una Vita Boema)
49: Universal Consciousness
(Coscienza Universale)
50: Relax
(Rilassarsi)

Pagan Street

(Via Pagana)

Who will you meet?
What will you say?
What will you do?
On Pagan Street.

Who will you *worship*?
Who will you *follow*?
Who will you *kiss*?
On Pagan Street.

Will it be the *Devil*?
Will it be *Lucifer*?
Will it be *Beelzebub*?
Who will you meet on Pagan Street?

Will you meet *Lilith*?
Will you meet the *"Sirens"*?
Will you meet the *"Temptress"*?
Who will you make LO♥E to, on Pagan Street?

What do you *bring*?
What do you *offer*?
What do you *sacrifice*?
On Pagan Street.

Will you sacrifice *yourself*?
Will you sacrifice your *life*?
Will you sacrifice your *dreams*?
Will you sacrifice your *hopes*?
Will you sacrifice your *mother*?
Will you sacrifice your *father*?
Will you sacrifice your *brother*?
Will you sacrifice your *sister*?
Will you sacrifice your LO♥ER?
On the altar of Pagan Street.

There's a lot of *people to meet.*
On Pagan Street.
There's a lot of *things to do.*
On Pagan Street.
There's *so much to see.*
On Pagan Street.

There will be *music.*
There will be *singers & dancers.*
There will be *acrobats & clowns.*
There's even going to be *fireworks.*
So...
...don't be late or you'll miss all the fun.

It's the *BEST place to be.*
It's the *ONLY place to be.*
On Pagan Street.

Bring your friends.
You're guaranteed a good time.
On Pagan Street.

"The Don"
31.03.2022

Adventures with my Father
(Avventure con mio Padre)

My father was called *Giuseppe Radice*.
But everyone called him *"Joe"*.
You've gotta understand that my father was a very strange man.
I could never figure him out.
He would do crazy shit that made absolutely no sense to me at all.
It must've made sense to him though, because when he had decided on something, he was committed to it.
There was nothing that would make him change his mind.
So...
...he liked to take me on adventures with him.

Now let me clarify, when I say *"adventures"*, I am using the world very loosely.
Actually, they were *"horror-shows"*, *nightmares*, in fact.
These adventures usually took place very early in the morning.
...very, very early in the morning.
...sometimes, 3:00am in the morning.
There was; going to the *"Fish Markets"* adventure.
There was; going to the *"Fruit Markets"* adventure @ 5:00am...
...a more civilised hour.
There was; going to buy the *"grapes for wine making"* adventure.
There was; going to buy *"live chickens at the Sydney Markets"* adventure.

In each case his strategy...
...his methodology was the same.

He had a fixed price in his head...
...above which he would not pay.

No matter what it was he had to buy.

He had done this, many times before.
He knew exactly what to do.
He was an expert.
A *"true"* professional.
No one could *"outwit"* him.
I wouldn't even attempt to try.

We would enter the markets & he would head to the stall he had always bought from before.
There he would get a *"benchmark"* price.
Then, & this is his strategy...
...he would check out the whole market comparing the price.
I, of course was his obedient, unwilling apprentice...
...following close behind him.
...making sure I kept up to his cracking pace.
...and he did set a cracking pace.
...scared that I would lose him amongst the melè of people.
...and believe me there were lots people.
...even at this *"ungodly"* hour.

Finally, after we had gone right around the whole market.
We would arrive back to the beginning.
For unsurprisingly, where we had started was our destination.
This is where he bought his goods.
This whole exercise had been a complete waste of time.
He could have bought the same goods right at the beginning.
...without walking right round the markets.
...but this was not for *"my"* father.
...he always liked to do things...
...his own way!

Finally, if that was not enough adventures for one morning...
...he'd say to me,
"Wait here, I won't be long. I'm just going off to do something."
("Aspetta qui. Vado a fare qualcosa. Retornerò presto.")
I REALLY used to hate this!
Who knows what that *"something"* was?
And he'd go off leaving me all alone.
These are the situations when time slows down to a crawl.
It seemed like an eternity before he came back.
And usually with no indication of where he'd been or what he'd done.

Oh yeah...
...I really LO♥ED having adventures with my father!

"The Don"
30.03.2022

Sins of the Father

(Peccati del Padre)

My father was a tyrant.
He was a patriarch.
He ruled with iron fists, literally.
He was very violent.
He was a bully.
He was aggressive.
I was afraid of him.
He scared me.
He owned me.
I lived in a prison.
I was a prisoner.

It never occurred to him that I didn't choose to be born.
That I had no choice in the matter.
That I was never asked, *"would you like to be born?"*
"Would you like to be the son of this man?"
Because if I was, my answer would definitely be, *"NO!"*
"Are you fucking made!"
"This guy's a fucking psycho!"
I never wanted to be his son.
I never wanted him as my father.
But I had no choice in the matter.
I was just his possession.
For him to do what he pleased.
He made me feel bad for being alive.
That I owed him.

So, he made me work.
He gave me all the *"shitty"* jobs.
...watering the garden.
...cleaning the chicken poo from the chicken pen.
...painting the roof of the garage on a hot day.
...cutting the grass with hand clippers.
...washing his beloved "Valiant".
...going to the markets with him @ 4 O'clock on a Saturday morning.
...helping reverse out of the garage @ 3:30am in the morning.
He used to start work very early in the mornings and he had great difficulty in reversing the car out of the garage.
The driveway was extremely narrow & there was a very acute bend that he had to negotiate.
And of course, this was made even more difficult because the car was a fucking monster.

A *"1969 Chrysler Valiant, Hemi 245Hp, V6 engine"*, for you, car enthusiasts.

It was a *"beast"*!
A real American petrol guzzler.
He loved it.
He loved it more than anything in the world.
Definitely more than my mother or me.

He hit me many times.
One time that I will never forget was when I was just 6 years old.
He hit me on my back with the end a belt.
I still have the marks to this very day.
I swore I would get my revenge one day.
And that day did eventually come.
I was 14 years old.
He was very angry at me...
...again, for some very stupid reason.
...in fact, he didn't even need a reason.
...I realised many years later that his anger had nothing to do with me.
...I was just a punching bag on which to release his frustrations.
Anyway, on this particular occasion I blew my fuse.
...I just saw *"red"*.
...I lost it.
As he was yelling & screaming at me, I punched him in the guts as hard as I could.
He dropped to his knees in front of me gasping for air.
I had winded him.
When he finally got air back into himself & stood up.
...he looked at me and said,
..."*I didn't think you'd have the guts!*"
"*What a FUCKING prick!*"
I thought to myself.

The day will always come when *"The sins of the father"* will be paid for.
It won't be immediate.
It may take time.
But they will be set straight.
And so, it happened for my father.
The day when he had to face his sins.

25th May, 2008...
...the day of his death!

I saw him die.
He did not have a good death!

"The Don"
31.03 2022

Are you FUCKING Kidding Me?

(Mi Stai CAZZO Prendendo in Giro?)

Are you FUCKING *weird?*
Are you FUCKING *joking?*
Are you FUCKING *crazy?*
Are you FUCKING *mad?*
Are you FUCKING *insane?*
Are you FUCKING *psycho?*
Are you FUCKING *balmy?*
Are you FUCKING *"out of your FUCKING mind"?*
Are you FUCKING *tripping?*
Are you FUCKING *"off this planet"?*
Are you FUCKING *stoopid?*
Are you FUCKING *fucked?*

Do me 2 favours...
...1 for me.
...and 1 for you.

And...
...by the way...
...get *FUCKED!*

Are you *FUCKING* kidding me?

"Are you cursing me?"
"No!"
"I'm just cursing to myself!"

"Nothing personal!"

Miriam + "The Don"
02.04.2022

I Am What I Am

(Sono Quello che Sono)

I do what I do.
I feel what I feel.
I think what I think.
I see what I see what I see.
I hear what I hear.
I LO❤E whom I LO❤E.

That's because...
...that's who I am.

I am what I am.
I've done ALL I can do.
There's nothing more I can do.

I've done ALL I could do.
There's nothing more I could do.

That's because...
...that's who I am.

I am what I am.

"The Don"
02.04.2022

She Saw Me

(Lei mi ha Visto)

I *had my guard down.*
I was *not expecting it.*
I was *exposed.*
I was *disarmed.*
I was *unexpecting it.*
I was *unprepared.*
I was *contemplative.*
I was *open.*
I was *vulnerable.*
I was *unnerved.*
I was *discombobulated.*

She saw *me.*
She saw *who I was.*
She *looked at me.*
She *knew.*
She *saw me.*
She saw me *with my guard down.*
She saw me *for who I really was.*

I winked at her.
What else could I do?
She walked past.
But...
...she saw me!

She saw who I was...
...who I REALLY was!

"The Don"
02.04.2022

Look but Do Not Touch

(Guarda ma non Toccare)

Look but do not touch.
Touch but do not feel.
Feel but do not taste.
Taste but do not shallow.
Shallow but do not enjoy.
Enjoy but do not LO♥E.
LO♥E but do not...
...be LO♥ED.

"The Don"
05.04.2022

I Am Not Participating
(Non sto Partecipando)

You want to touch me...
...but
I am not participating.
You want to hug me...
...but
I am not participating.
You want to hold me...
...but
I am not participating.
You want to kiss me...
...but
I am not participating.
You want to sleep with me...
...but
I am not participating.
You want to have sex with me...
...but
I am not participating.
You want to fuck me...
...but
I am not participating.
You want to make LO❤E to me...
...but
I am not participating.

"The Don"
05.04.2022

The Answers to Everything & Nothing
(Le Risposte a Tutto e Niente)

Are you *asking questions?*
Do you *want answers?*
Do you know what you're *looking for?*
Do you know what you *want?*
Are you a *seeker?*
Are you a *searcher?*
Are you on a *journey?*
Are you on a *quest?*

What do you *seek?*
What do you *want?*
What are you *looking for?*
What are you *hoping to find?*

You've come to the *right place.*
You are *here.*
This is the end of your *journey.*
This is your *final destination.*
Here lies the answers to everything & nothing!

"The Don"
08.04.2022

Adaptation

(Adattamento)

Can you *bend?*
Can you *accommodate?*
Can you *change?*
Can you *transform?*
Can you *evolve?*
Can you *rebel?*
Can you be *fluidic?*
Can you be *flexible?*
Can you *negotiate?*
Can you be *non-judgemental?*
Can you *adapt?*

Are you *stoic?*
Are you *inflexible?*
Are you *rigid?*
Are you *fixed?*
Are you *stagnant?*
Are you *stuck?*
Are you *conservative?*
Are you *adaptable?*

Change, evolve adapt!

"The Don"
09.04.2022

I Want YOU!

(Voglio TE!)

That's what she has to say.
That's the only thing I want to hear.
There is nothing more to be said.
There is nothing more to say.
That's all she has to say...
...."I want YOU!"

I can't continue on this way.
I cannot keep doing this.
I must stop it.
I must put an end to it.
The only thing that would change my mind would be if she says...
...."I want YOU!"

There's nothing more to be said.
There's nothing more to be done.
The story has come to an end.
The book is closed.
Unless she says...
...."I want you!"

...."I want you!"
"So bad!"
"Oh, baby"...
...."I want YOU!"

Which won't happen!

"The Don"
10.04.2022

Who's Gonna Occupy This Chair?
(Chi Occuperà Questa Sedia?)

Who's gonna sit in this chair...
...now that you're gone?
Who's goanna sit opposite me?
Will you excite me?
Are you gonna challenge me?
Am I gonna challenge you?
What new adventures are in store for this chair?
What new adventures are in store for me?

For whomever sits in this chair...
...they will definitely be a new story.
A new adventure.
Maybe...
...it'll be you who will sit on this chair.

"The Don"
10.04.2022

Rejected & Abandoned Once Again

(Rifiutato e Abbandonato di Nuovo)

I thought I was *over it*.
I thought I had *dealt with it*.
I thought I had *overcome it*.
I thought I had *conquered it*.
But I was wrong.
Oh, was I so wrong?
Because, I was...
...rejected & abandoned once again.
And the suffering was excruciating.

I was thrown out like a *"dirty shirt"*.
I was in a *heap of hurt*.
I *lost it*.
I *panicked*.
I *started sweating*.
I *went white as a ghost*.
I *felt all my blood drain out of me*.
I *became lifeless*.
Because, I was...
...rejected & abandoned once again.

My emotions went *crazy*.
My head was *spinning*.
My mouth became *parched*.
My heart was beating at *100km/hr*.
My brain had become *mush*.
Because, I was...
...rejected & abandoned once again.

I wanted to *escape*.
I wanted to *disappear*.
I wanted *to run away*.
I wanted to *get out of there as fast as I could*.
I wanted to *DIE!*
Because, I was...
...rejected & abandoned once again.

The 27th of March, 2022
One of the worst nights of my Life!

I should NEVER have gone out with her that night!
Because, I was...
...rejected & abandoned once again. "The Don", 11.04.2022

Time to SHOUT!

(È Ora di Gridare!)

Time to be *quiet is over.*
Time to be *silent has finished.*
Time to *keep your mouth closed is no more.*
Time to *sit & do nothing is well & truly over.*
Because...
...it's time to SHOUT!

Time to sit on your *hands is over.*
Time to sit on your *arse is finished.*
Time to *just accept things has passed.*
Time to *think that things will be better is gone.*
Because...
...it's time to SHOUT!

Time to *do something has arrived.*
Time to *get vocal is here.*
Time to *make a noise is required.*
Time to *protest is here.*
Because...
...it's time to SHOUT!

Time to *get rid of these ARSEHOLES in power.*
Time to *make changes is here.*
Time to *rebel has arrived.*
Time to *be revolutionary is now.*
So...
...it's time to SHOUT!

Time to *get rid of these FUCKING idiots.*
Time to *change the system!*
Time to *kick out these stupid fools.*
Time *for a RÉVOLUTION!*
It's time to SHOUT!

"The Don"
14.04.2022

Peace, LO♥E & Harmony
(Pace, Amor e Armonia)

Peace, LO♥E & Harmony to everyone!

"The Don"
14.04.2022

The Crucible

(Il Crogiolo)

Who is coming?
Where will I be sitting?
Can I bring a friend?
What time does it start?
What is the topic?
Do I need to bring anything to the next meeting of...
..."The Crucible"?

What do you do there?
What do you discuss?
Is the coffee any good?
How many people usually come along?
Can I come?
Can I join…
...."The Crucible"?

We discuss many issues here...
...Philosophy.
...politics.
...health.
...art.
...culture.
...music.
...LO♥E.
...the meaning of LIFE.
at...
...."The Crucible".
...and many other issues.

It's a *"think tank"*.
It's a *"melting pot"*.
It's a *"confluence of ideas"*.
It's a *"joining of souls"*.
So, yes do come along to...
..."The Crucible".

Where do I find...
...*"The Crucible"*?
It's right next door to *"Galuzzo's Fruit shop & Deli"*.
You can't miss it.
Every morning we are there.
Inside...
...*"The Crucible"*.

(Dedicated to "Joe Galuzzo")

"The Don"
15 04.2022

The Last Supper
(L'ultima Cena)

What's on the menu?
Who's gonna be there?
Where is it gonna be?
Should I bring something?
To the last supper.

Will there be any music?
Will there be any dancing?
Will there be any singing?
Will there be any drinking?
At the last supper.

Is it a formal occasion?
Is it a *"black tie"* event?
Is it casual dress?
Can I bring a friend?
To the last supper.

How long will it go on for?
Will it go past midnight?
How many people are gonna be there?
Will I know anyone there?
At the last supper.

Will there be a ritual?
Will there be a sacrifice?
Will there be a *"Happening"*?
Will there be a ceremony?
At the last supper.

"The Don"
16.04.2022

I've Got Your Back
(Ti Guardo le Spalle)

Don't worry *about a thing*.
Do worry if you *make a mistake*.
Don't worry if you *have an accident*.
Don't worry if you *get sick*.
Don't worry if you have *no food*.
Don't worry if you have *no money*.
Don't worry if you have *no place to stay*.
Don't worry if *the one you LO♥E rejects you*.
Don't worry *about a thing*.
Because...
...*I've got your back*.

I'll always be there for you.
To *save you*.
To *protect you*.
To *keep you safe*.
To *keep you warm*.
To *LO♥E you*.
Because...
...*I've got your back*.

You can *count on me*.
You can *rely on me*.
You can *depend on me*.
I won't let you down.
I'll always be there for you.
Whenever you need me.
Because...
...*I've got your back*.

"The Don"
16.04.2022

She Was Not a Good Friend

(Non era Una Buona Amica)

She said she was my friend.
And that may be true.
She said I was her *"Angel"*
And that may be true.
She said that she LO♥ED me.
And that may be true.
But...
...she was not a good friend.

She never *"had my back"*.
She never *listened to me.*
She never *held me.*
She never *protected me.*
She never *cared for me.*
She never *cared about me.*
She never *kissed me.*
She never *fucked me.*
She never *LO♥ED me.*
She never made *LO♥E to me.*
She was not a good friend.

"The Don"
16.04.2022

Time Heals All Wounds

(Il tempo Guarisce Tutte le Ferite)

It's a process.
That's for sure.
How long?
How long is a piece of string?
Who knows?
It could be a short time.
It could be a long time.
I guess it depends on the severity of the wound.
Is it just a superficial, surface wound?
Or...
...is it a deep cut?
...one that has gone right to the bone?
This is probably the hardest to heal.
And will probably take the most time to heal.
Maybe, a very long time.
There's nothing much you can do about.
You try your best not to think about it.
You try to keep yourself busy.
You go out.
You meet new people.
You have a good time.
But when you are in those moments…
The wound will resurface.
The hurt will be felt again.
You try consciously to remove these memories from you mind.
You try very hard to switch off your brain.
Good luck, I say to you.
But eventually...
...over time.
...*time heals all wounds.*

I think this time, time will take a long time to heal!

"The Don"
17.04.2022

If You Can't Make LO♥E to the One You LO♥E, Make LO♥E to the One You're With!

(Se non riesci a fare l'amore con colui che ami,
Fai l'AMORE con la persona con cui stai!)

If You Can't Make LO♥E to the One You LO♥E,
Make LO♥E to the One You're With!

Women FUCK whomever they want.
Men FUCK whomever they can get!

"The Don"
18.04.2022

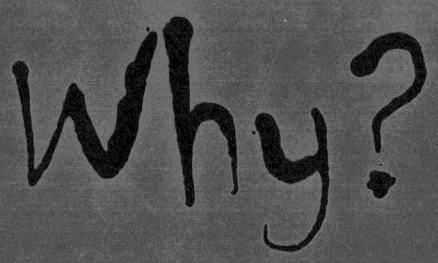

(Come mai?)

Why?

Why not?

Oh, FUCK off!

"The Don"
20.04.2022

My Mother, Angela
(Mia madre, Angela)

My mother is called *Angela, Angela Martone*.
Angela means *angel* & *Martone* means *hammer*, in Italian.
And no truer name describes my mother best than Angel.
She is truly a sweet angel.
Kind of heart.
Warm of spirit.
And generous to the core.

She was born in a small village called *"San Fele"*, in the southern region of Italy called *"Basilicata"*.
She was born on the 5th May, 1932.
Her father (my grandfather) was called *Vito Martone*, after whom I was named.
They lived on a farm in area called *"Palazzulo"*.
She tells me she had a wonderful childhood.

This all ended abruptly when she got married at the tender age of just 18 years of age.
In those days marriages were negotiated between families.
There was no love involved.
He was 26 years old, 8 years older than her.
His name was *Giuseppe Radice*.
My father.

Radice means *"roots"* in Italian.
The roots of a tree.
Strong, dependable, unswerving, steadfast & resilient.
The *"Radices"* were from the land, of the land & worked the land.
They were tough, hard people.
They had no time for frivolous activities.
"Hard work" was their mantra & my mother was put to work as soon as she set foot on the *"Radice"* farm called *"La Difesa"*.

She told me once that she went from *"Heaven to Hell"*.
I asked her why did her father marry her off to my father.
Her reply was that her father apologised to her.
Apparently, he said to her, *"I'm sorry, I didn't know they were like that!"*

She lived with him for 57 years.
And when he died on the 25th May 2008...
...I was driving her back home (just me & her), in the car...
...right in front of the house, the family house in Five Dock...
...where she still lives...
...she SCREAMED...
..."I AM FREE AT LAST!"
..."I licked his FUCKING arse for 57 years"...
..."and now I can FUCKING do whatever I want!"
And I said to her...
..."Mum this is your time!"

(Dedicated to my mother, Angela Martone)

"The Don"
21.04.2022

I Know You're Lonely

(So che sei solo)

You hide behind your tough outer shell.
Your façade is there to protect you…
To show others that you are tough.
That no one can FUCK with you…
…unless you want them to.
That you don't need anybody.
That you don't need anyone.
That you are independent.
That you are strong.

You are very smart.
No one can pull the wool over your eyes.
You are no one's fool.
No one can FUCK around with you.
You have their measure…
…and much more.
You can run rings around everyone.
You have everything planned…
…beforehand.
This is your strategy.
This is your weapon.
This is your defence.

But I've seen behind that shell.
I've seen behind that façade.
I've seen you naked *(metaphorically speaking, of course)*.
I've seen who you really are.
An innocent, small, lonely, scared little girl.
One that has been abused.
One that has never really been LO♥ED.
One that has never really felt REAL LO♥ED.
That's who you really are…
…deep inside.

I've seen your loneliness.
I've seen your emptiness.
I've seen your NEED for LO♥E.
I've seen who you REALLY are...
...deep inside.

I know that you're lonely.

"The Don"
21.04.2022

I Want to be LO♥ED

(Voglio essere Amato)

Is that too much to ask?
To be LO♥ED...
... for who I am.

Apparently so!

"The Don"
21.04.2022

Cunt, is not a Dirty Word (revisited)

(Figa, non è una Sporca Parola (rivisitato))

Cunt, is not a dirty word!
Cunt, is not a dirty word!
Cunt, is not a dirty word!
Don't you believe what you've seen or you've heard.

Cunt, is not a dirty word!
Cunt, is not a dirty word!
Cunt, is not a dirty word!
Don't you believe what you've seen or you've heard.
Cunt, is not a dirty word!

"The Don"
26.04.2022

Exclusivity

(Esclusività)

Are you a one person LO♥ER?
Or...
...do you like to *share the LO♥E?*
Do like to be *attached?*
Do you like to be *owned?*
Do you like you be *possessed?*
Do you like to be *an object?*
Do you like to be *a "sex" object?*
Do you like to be *used?*
Do you like to *use?*
Do you like to *FUCK?*
Do you like to be *FUCKED?*
Do you like to be a *"FUCKABLE" object?*
Do you like to be a *"piece of meat"?*
Do you like to *be LO♥ED?*
Do you like *to LO♥E?*
Do you like *"Exclusivity"?*
I say...
...FUCK "Exclusivity"!

Live in *"the moment".*
Enjoy *"the moment".*
Be in *"the moment".*
LO♥E in *"the moment".*
LO♥E *the one you're with.*
FUCK "Exclusivity"!

"Exclusivity" is not all it's cracked up to be!

"The Don"
28.04.2022

The Sex, LO♥E Dichotomy
(La Dicotomia Sesso, Amore)

Do you live a *double life?*
Do have an *"alter ego"*?
A second *"persona"*?
Maybe, multiple *"personas"*?
Do you separate sex & LO♥E?
Do you LO♥E the one you're having sex with?
Do you LO♥E the one you're FUCKING?
Maybe they're just *"friends with benefits"*?
Maybe, they're just a *"good FUCK"*?
Maybe, they're just *"easy"*?
Maybe, you're just *"easy"*?
Maybe, it's just *"easy"*?
Whatever it is?
This is the "Sex, LO♥E Dichotomy".

Where do you stand?

"The Don"
28.04.2022

The Third Person
(La Terza Persona)

I don't wanna be your *"patsy"*.
I don't wanna be your *"cuckold"*.
I don't wanna be your *"clown"*.
I don't wanna be your *"lacky"*.
I don't wanna be your *"plaything"*.
I don't wanna be your *"toy"*.
I don't want to be your *"puppet on a string"*.
I don't wanna be your *"shoulder to cry on"*.
I don't wanna be your *"pin cushion"*.
I don't wanna be your *"backstop"*.
I don't wanna be your *"Godfather"*.
I don't wanna be your *"third person"*!

"The Don"
28.04.2022

The Noise of Silence

(Il Rumore del Silenzio)

Silence is *LOUD*.
Silence is *deafening*.
Silence is *noisy*.
Silence *hurts my ears*.
Silence *speaks volumes*.
Silence *speaks all languages*.
Silence is *musical*.
Silence is *threatening*.
Silence is *whimsical*.
Silence is *violent*.
Silence is *romantic*.
Silence *cuts like a knife*.
Silence *kills*.
Silence has *no tongue*.
Silence has *no mouth*.
Silence has *no time*.
Silence is *old*.
Silence *never gets old*.
Silence is *ageless*.
Silence *will never DIE*.
Silence is *DEATH*.
Silence is *POWER*.
Silence is the *voice of the VOICELESS*.

This is the *POWER of silence*.

This is the *noise of silence*.

"The Don"
29.04.2022

The Power Paradox
(Il Paradosso del Potere)

Do not seek power & you will be *powerful*.
Do not seek to control & you will be *uncontrollable*.
This is the "Power Paradox".

He who seeks power is *weak*.
He who seeks to control is *full of fear*.
He who seeks to manipulate is *selfish*.
He who seeks immortality fears *DEATH*.
He who seeks DEATH fears *LIFE*.
This is the "Power Paradox".

This is the *"Ying & Yang"* of the Universe.
Power is gained by NOT seeking it.
This is the "Power Paradox".

"The Don"
29.04.2022

Lean on Me

(Affidati a Me)

We all need someone we can *feed on.*
We all need someone we can *sit on.*
We all need someone we can *sleep on.*
We all need someone we can *dream on.*
We all need someone we can *cream on.*
We all need someone we can *LO♥E on.*
We all need someone we can *BLEED on.*
We all need someone we can *lean on.*

Well, if you wanna, you can *feed on me.*
Well, if you wanna, you can *sit on me.*
Well, if you wanna, you can *sleep on me.*
Well, if you wanna, you can *dream on me.*
Well, if you wanna, you can *cream on me.*
Well, if you wanna, you can *LO♥E on me.*
Well, if you wanna, you can *BLEED on me.*
Well, if you wanna, you can *lean on me.*

"The Don"
29.04.2022

LO♥E is a Dirty Word

(L'AMORE è una Parola Sporca)

Don't *seek it*.
Don't *look for it*.
Don't *search for it*.
Don't *pine for it*.
Don't *want it*.
Don't *think it*.
Don't *say it*.
Don't *utter it*.
And certainly...
...don't *feel it!*
Because...
...LO♥E is a, dirty word.

Believe what you've seen & you've heard.
Because...
...LO♥E is a, dirty word.

LO♥E is a, dirty word.

"The Don"
30.04.2022

Don't Verbal Me

(Non Parlarmi)

Don't *talk down at me.*
Don't *lecture me.*
Don't *put words into my mouth.*
Don't *shout at me.*
Don't *yell at me.*
Don't *harangue me.*
Don't *bamboozle me.*
Don't *trick me.*
Don't tell me *what to say.*
Don't tell me *that you know BETTER than me.*
Don't tell me *that you're an "EXPERT".*
Don't tell me *what to think.*
Don't tell me *what to feel.*
Don't tell *whom to be.*
Don't tell *me LIES.*
Don't tell me *SHIT.*
Don't verbal me.

Because...
...I am one of the VOICELESS.

Hard for you to accept but...
...I DO have my own VOICE.
I can SPEAK for myself.
I DON'T need you to talk for me

"The Don"
30.04.2022

All Things Have an End
(Tutte le cose hanno una Fine)

That is the law of the Universe.
That is the nature of things.
Nothing lasts forever.
In fact...
...there is no forever.
There is just *"the here & now"*.
Nothing else exist.
It is all imaginary.
It is all an illusion.
Because...
...*all things have an end.*

LO♥*E* has an end
Life has an end.
Humanity has an end.
The Earth has an end.
The Sun has an end
The Solar System has an end.
The galaxy has an end.
Even the Universe has an end.
Because...
...*all things have an end.*

Accept that undeniable reality...
... *all things have an end.*
Even *you*.

"The Don"
30.04.2022

I'm Gonna Use Her Words Back at Her
(Userò le Sue Sarole Contro di Lei)

Yes...
...that's what she said.
"What's up?"
I'm gonna use her words back at her.
"You're not my style".
I'm gonna use her words back at her.
"You're too old for me!"
I'm gonna use her words back at her.
"You're too easy!"
I'm gonna use her words back at her.
"You're a romantic!"
I'm gonna use her words back at her.
"You're too emotional!"
I'm gonna use her words back at her.
"You're too sensitive!"

I'm gonna use her words back at her.

"The Don"
30.04.2022

The Future

(Il Futuro)

The Future is what we make of it.
The Future is what we want of it.
The Future is mine.
The Future is yours.
The Future is ours.
The Future is here.
The Future is right now.
The Future is everywhere.
The Future cannot be escaped.
The Future is everything.
The Future is open.
The Future is ALL.

"The Don"
03.05.2022

ACCESS

(Accesso)

You give me access to everything else...
...yet...
...you won't give me access to your body!

"The Don"
03.05.2022

Adversity Brought Us Together

(Le Avversità ci hanno Uniti)

Adversity brought us together.
LO♥E tore us apart.

"The Don"
04.05.2022

Let's Stand Naked Together

(Restiamo Nudi Insieme)

Let's face *each other*.
Let's face *our fears*.
Let's face *society*.
Let's face *the world*.
Let's face *the Universe*.
Let's face *the Cosmos*.
Let's stand naked together...
...hand in hand.

We have nothing to *hide*.
We have nothing to *conceal*.
We'll stand naked *together*.
Let's stand naked together...
...hand in hand.

Nothing will *hurt us*.
Nothing will *destroy us*.
Let's stand naked together...
...hand in hand.

We have nothing to *fear*.
Not even death can *hurt us*.
When we stand naked together.

We are *invincible*.
We are *indestructible*.
We are *powerful*.
We are *one*.
We are the Universe.
Let's stand naked together.

"The Don"
04.05.2022

You are Boring

(Sei Noioso)

You have nothing to say.
You speak in clichès.
Your poor attempt at jokes are not funny.
You actually don't have a sense of humour.
You are boring!

You don't do anything interesting.
You have nothing interesting to say.
You live a boring existence.
You have no life.
You are boring!

You say the same things.
You do the same things.
You have no curiosity.
You have no interests.
You are boring!

You don't sing.
You don't dance.
You don't party.
Your ideas are boring *(you have no ideas)*.
Your friends are boring *(you have no friends)*.
Your life is boring *(you have no life)*.
You are boring!

Boring!

Boring!

Boring!

Boring!

You are boring!

I would rather shoot myself rather than spend time with you!

"The Don"
06.05.2022

Template

(Modello)

I've created the template.
I've set the form.
I've made a garden.
I've planted the seeds.
I've established an environment.
You've seen it grow.
You've felt its energy.
You've been enveloped by its warmth.
You've been held in its arms.
You've been cuddled in its warm embrace.
You've enjoyed what it has to offer.
You've liked it...
...a lot!
You've come back for more...
...many times.
You know what to expect.
So, it's nothing new for you.

Because...
...I've created the template.

I have your tobacco!
Will you come back?
I have your music book!
Will you come back?

Because...
...I've created the template.

"The Don"
06.05.2022

I Have Clean Sheets
(Ho Lenzuola Pulite)

Do you want to get HIGH?
I have clean sheets.
Do you want stay with me?
I have clean sheets.
Do you wanna sleep with me tonight?
I have clean sheets.
Do you want to taste me?
I have clean sheets.
Do you want to feel me?
I have clean sheets.
Do you want to FUCK?
I have clean sheets.
Do want to make LO♥E with me?
I have clean sheets.

"The Don"
06.05.2022

Everyone Lies

(Tutti Bugie)

You lie.
I lie.
Everyone lies.
We ALL lie.
Let's admit it.
Everyone lies.

I'm lying right now.
Yep...
...everyone lies.

All are lies.
Lies are everywhere.
Lies fill the air.
We breathe in all those lies.
We are filled with lies.
Because...
...everyone lies.

Your parents lie.
Your friends lie.
Politicians lies.
Religions lie.
Society lies.
Everyone lies.

That's the truth!
Everyone lies.

"The Don"
06.05.2022

The End

(La Fine)

Some say that *"The End"* is just a *new beginning*.
Some say that *"The End"* is a *time to start a new*.
Some say that *"The End"* is a *new start*.
Some say that *"The End"* is *starting over*.
Some say that *"The End"* is a *new Future*.
Some say that *"The End"* is an *opportunity to start a fresh*.
Some say *"The End"* is a *"Rebirth"*.
Some say there is an *"Afterlife"*.
Some say there is a *"Heaven"*.
Some say there is a *"Hell"*.
Some say *"The End"* is a *new dimension*.
Some say *"The End"* is a *new reality*.
Some say *"The End"* is a *portal into another universe*.

I say "The End"...
...is just "The End".

It's just "The End"!

And that's "The End"!

"The Don"
06.05.2022

Give Me Some Validation
(Dammi Qualche Conferma)

Give me some *recognition*.
I am not *invisible*.
I am not *nothing*.
I *exist*.
I am *someone*.
So...
...please, give me some validation.

Give me some *praise*.
I am *here*.
Can you *see* me?
Can you *hear* me?
Can you *feel* me?
I *exist*.
I am *someone*.
So...
...*give me some validation*.

Give me some *kindness*.
Can you see my *pain*?
Can you hear my *cries*?
Can you feel my *suffering*?
I am *human*.
I *exist*.
I am *someone*.
So...
...*give me some validation*.

Give me some *acknowledgement*.
That's all I *need*.
That's all I *want*.
That's all *we need*.
That's all *we want*.
Sometimes...
Because…
...I *exist*.
...I am *someone*.
So...
...please, give me some validation.

"The Don"
09.05.2022

Do Not Expect Anything & Get Everything
(Non Aspettarti Nulla e Ottieni Tutto)

Do not expect anything & get everything!

"The Don"
09.05.2022

A Bohemian Life

(Una Vita Boema)

I want to live a *"Bohemian Life"*.
Live in *Paris*.
Stroll along the *Seine*.
Have an expresso in *Montmartre*.
Drop into the *Louvre*.
See *"La Gioconda"* for the millionth time.
Walk into the *"Pompidou Centre"*.

I want to live a *"Bohemian Life"*.
I want to write poetry on the *"Champs-Élysées"*.

"The Don"
14.03.2022

Universal Consciousness

(Coscienza Universale)

It's about *time*.
It's about *space*.
It's about the *entire human race*.
It's about *"Universal Consciousness"*.

It's about *connecting*.
It's about *empathy*.
It's about *feeling*.
It's about *belonging*.
It's about *"Universal Consciousness"*.

It's about *seeing*.
It's about *hearing*.
It's about *beauty*.
It's about *"The Light"*.
It's about *LIFE*.
It's about *"Universal Consciousness"*.

It's about *appreciation*.
It's about *recognising*.
It's about *perception*.
It's about *LO*❤*E*.
It's about *"Universal Consciousness"*.

It's about *you*.
It's about *me*.
It's about the *whole human race*.
It's about *NATURE*.
It's about *EVERYTHING*.
It's about *"Universal Consciousness"*.

"The Don"
16.05.2022

Relax

(Rilassarsi)

Just relax.
Take it easy.
Don't stress out.
Don't think too much.
Just let things happen.
Be cool.
Be chilled.
Be easy.
That's all you have to do.
Things will take care of themselves.
You don't need to force anything.
Just relax.

Be cool.
Everything will work out just fine.
Enjoy yourself.
Enjoy the ride.
Have fun.
Be cool.
Relax.

Just relax.

"The Don"
17.05.2022

Leslie

Books written by "The Don"

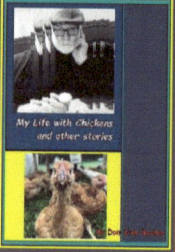
"My Life with Chickens & other stories: I Pity the Poor Immigrant"
Published:
10th September, 2019
Autobiography Book 1:
0 – 12 years old

"Poems for Misfits, Miscreants, Misanthropes, Mavericks, Losers & Malcontents!"
Published:
10th June, 2020
Book of Poems 1

"Poems for Troubled Minds & Trouble Hearts"
Published:
10th August, 2020

Book of Poems 2

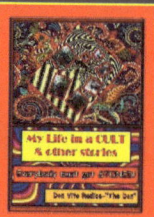
"My Life in a CULT & other stories: Everybody Must Get STONED!"
Published:
10th September, 2020
Autobiography Book 2:
15 – 30 years old

"Poems for Restless Minds & Restless Hearts"
Published:
10th October, 2020
Book of Poems 3

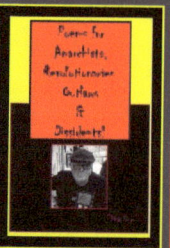
"Poems for Anarchists, Revolutionaries, Outlaws & Dissidents!"
Published:
10th November, 2020

Book of Poems 4

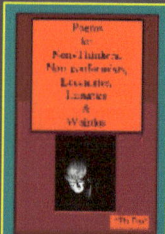
"Poems for Non-Thinkers & Eccentrics"
Published:
10th December, 2020
Book of Poems 5

"The Rantings of a Madman"
Published:
10th January, 2021

Book of Poems 6

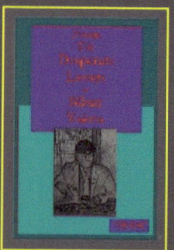
"Poems for Desperate Lovers & Silent Voices"
Published:
10th February, 2021
Book of Poems 7

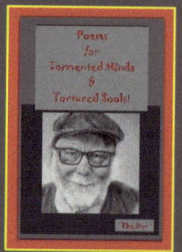
"Poems for Tormented Minds & Tortured Souls"
Published:
10th March, 2021
Book of Poems 8

All available ONLY online

Books written by "The Don"

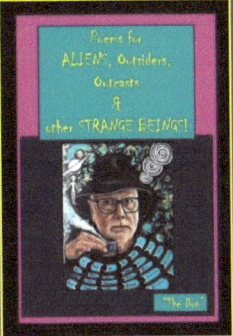

"Poems for ALIENS, Outsiders, Outcasts & other STRANGE BEINGS!"
Published: 10th April, 2021
Book of Poems 9

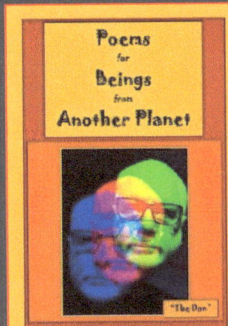

"Poems for Beings From Another Planet"
Published: 10th May, 2021
Book of Poems 10

"Poems for Mindless Beings & Lost Souls"
Published: 10th June, 2021
Book of Poems 11

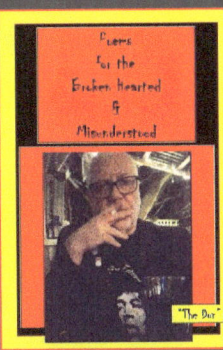

"Poems for the Broken Hearted & Misunderstood
Published: 10th July, 2021
Book of Poems 12

"Poems for Poems for the Bewildered, Dazed & Confused"
10th August, 2021
Book of Poems 13

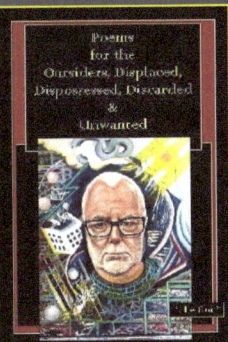

"Poems for the Outsiders, Displaced, Dispossessed, Discarded & Unwanted"
Published: 10th Sept, 2021
Book of Poems 14

All available ONLY online

"Poems for Secret Agents, Phantom Agents, Agents of Change, Agent Provocateurs & Agents of Chaos"
Published: 10th Oct, 2021
Book of Poems 15

"Poems for Disenchanted, Disillusioned & Delusional"
Published: 10th November, 2021
Book of Poems 16

Books written by "The Don"

"Poems for the Stoners, drugos, ACID takers & Psychedelic LO❤ERS (Everybody Must Get Stoned)"
Published: 10th December, 2021
Book of Poems 17

"Poems for Anarchists, Rebels & Revolutionaries
Published: 10th January, 2022
Book of Poems 18

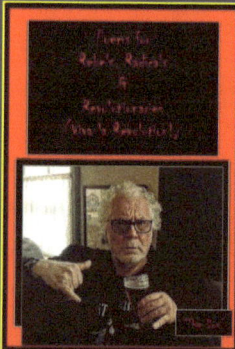

"Poems for Rebels, Radicals & Revolutionaries (Viva la Révolution!)"
Published: 10th February, 2022
Book of Poems 19

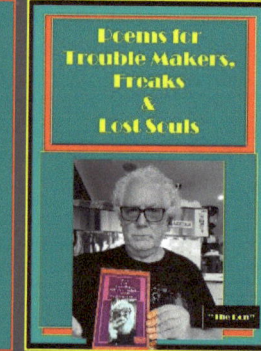

"Poems for Trouble Makers, Freaks & Lost Souls"
Published: 10th March 2022
Book of Poems 20

"Poems for Zombies & the Walking Dead"
Published: 10th April 2022
Book of Poems 21

"Poems for Non-Conformists (Never conform!)"
Published: 10th May 2022
Book of Poems 22

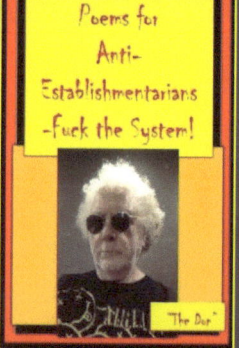

"Poems for Anti-Establishment-arians -Fuck the System!"
Published: 10th June 2022
Book of Poems 23

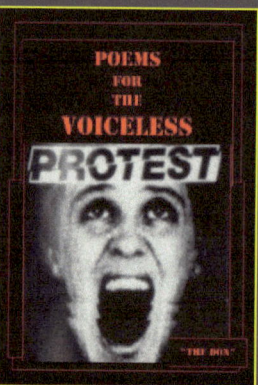

"Poems for the Voiceless"
Published: 10th July 2022
Book of Poems 24

All available ONLY online

www.ingramcontent.com/pod-product-compliance
Lightning Source LLC
Chambersburg PA
CBHW042048290426
44109CB00006B/149